First Grade Sentence STARTERS

Mark Linley

Dedicated to all teachers
and to the children in their care

A special thanks to all of the wonderful artists on Etsy who contributed to this publication:

Emily Peterson Studio
LePetiteMarket
Yene Design
My Cutie Store
Digital Art Cart
Cliparts Store

Doodles First
Nana Vics Digitals
Crafty Clipart
Graphic Passion
Luminarium Graphics

ISBN 978-0-9977255-8-2

Contact:
Mark Linley
bartlebysbox@gmail.com

CONTENTS

A Word from the Author About First Grade Sentence STARTERS

The reproducible pages in this book consist entirely of open-ended writing prompts for first grade writers. These writing prompts have been highly productive in my own first grade teaching practice, and I have been consistently amazed over the years at both the quality and sheer variety of the writing my students have produced in response to them.

First Grade Sentence Starters work because they invite students to think. They invite students to reflect deeply upon themselves and the world around them, and they give students the freedom to respond in their own unique and wonderful ways, both in writing and illustration. These sentence starters will prompt rich, insightful, thought-provoking, touching, and perhaps even startling pieces of writing from your students. They will free your students to express themselves in a multitude of ways. They will elicit deep powerful statements from your students, giving you insight into your students' lives.

This is the power of the open-ended sentence starters. They give students the freedom to express their thoughts, feelings, beliefs, knowledge, interests, and hopes without the somewhat arbitrary restraints of writing tasks that demand specific content criteria for the satisfactory completion of written assignments. The use of *First Grade Sentence Starters* will result in excellent student writing.

Think of them as art or illustrated poetry, as enduring expressive recordings of the lives your students live, to share with family and friends, as something to keep.

Enjoy.

How to Use this Book

Purpose

The intention of *First Grade Sentence Starters* is to invite students to think, to reflect upon their lives and the world around them, and to express these reflections in writing and illustration. *First Grade Sentence Starters* are designed to help teachers teach their students to create meaningful writing.

Flexibility

There are many ways in which *First Grade Sentence Starters* may be used - in whole group and in small group, integrated into thematic units and as stand-alone writing prompts, and for use in class and as homework.

Teachers collect, even curate many materials over time to assist in the planning and teaching of curricula. They integrate these materials into their practice in myriad ways. Certainly, a teacher may use *First Grade Sentence Starters* in conjunction with other curricular content. A *First Grade Sentence Starter* may be used as follow-up to a read-aloud on a particular topic - fear, for example, in *There's Something in My Attic*, by Mercer Mayer. A prompt about love or duty or belief could fit nicely into a thematic unit on family, to give another example. The *Index of First Lines* will help you to find pages appropriate to the content you are teaching.

A teacher may also use *First Grade Sentence Starters* as stand-alone, straight out of the box, independent writing lessons irrespective of other curricular goals. *First Grade Sentence Starters* can also be sent as homework, where they serve to engage families in deep powerful discussions. My experience has been that parents appreciate thoughtful homework assignments. Your students will be proud of the work they produce.

Instruction

A teacher may begin to teach writing by having students dictate what they want to write. A student dictates to the teacher what he or she wants to write and the teacher writes it down for the child to copy. This takes surprisingly little time, actually. At first, because students are unfamiliar with the process, it may take a couple of minutes per student, some less, some more; but once students come to know what is expected of them, the time is reduced dramatically, to ten seconds for some children. Of course, more time can always be spent talking with a student about the his or her writing, leading the child to a better expression of what he or she intends.

Sometimes I will spend extended periods of time conversing with students about their writing, talking them through their thoughts and language, transcribing what they say onto the pages they write. Peer-sharing is especially useful for getting students to know what to write before they begin to write and before they conference with the teacher. Meanwhile, teachers show students during discussion periods how to speak in complete sentences and how to judge the quality of their sentences based on the use of details, the vocabulary employed, the story content, the ideas expressed, the images portrayed, the originality, etc.

Alternatively, a teacher may ask the entire class to copy a sentence from the board. Advanced and enthusiastic students can begin to write a second sentence on their own as other students finish copying the first sentence. (All *First Grade Sentence Starters* have enough space for two sentences). Many students will spend significant time working on their illustrations. The teacher and other adults in the room move from student to student correcting spelling, making comments, asking questions, and taking dictation from individual students and writing it down for students to copy as second sentences.

Sometimes it will take two or more writing sessions for students to complete a single piece of writing. It is important to allow students to complete their writing, even if it takes longer than expected. It is better to have one complete piece of writing than to have two incomplete pieces of writing. Forego giving a second writing assignment to slower writers in the interest of allowing such students the extra time they need to complete the first writing assignment. Faster students can move on as slower students continue to work. The same *First Grade Sentence Starter* can be given to students more than once. Completed writing can be collected over time and stapled together into little books and sent home to read with families and to keep.

Invented Spelling and Phonemic Awareness

First Grade children begin to write when they understand that words are made of sounds and that these sounds can be represented with letters. Once children begin to orally segment words into their individual sounds they then want to write the words down. At the beginning, the words they write down may consist of only the first letter, or perhaps the first and last letters only. As students become more and more phonemically aware, they are able to capture more and more sounds in the words they write. These writings will be misspelled according to convention but will function well to convey meaning. This is what is called inventive spelling.

Children typically learn how to spell most words gradually, with a combination of sight memory and phonemic reasoning. For example, a child might learn how to spell a word such as *playground* like this:

pagd - plagd - playgrd - playgrond - playgrowund - playground

Some children may be able to memorize a word right away or with few errors. Other children will only gradually accumulate the bits and pieces of a word's conventional spelling, eventually learning how to spell it after reading it many times and after attempting to spell it inventively on many occasions over time.

Many of the pages of *First Grade Sentence Starters* feature words that may be difficult to sound-out for first graders; others contain CVC words and high frequency words only. Writing should always be taught in tandem with reading instruction. The role of *First Grade Sentence Starters* is not to teach word decoding, but rather to teach the essential writing practice of producing meaningful writing. Invented spelling is an essential part of this process and phonemic awareness is its prerequisite.

Results

With consistent phonemic awareness instruction and regular writing practice your students will become progressively better at using these truly deep, open-ended writing prompts to express themselves. By the end of the year following a fairly rigorous early literacy reading and writing program where students are taught the fundamentals of decoding, inventive spelling, and phonemic awareness, you will find that most of your students will be writing freely and well on their way to academic success.

Name ---------------------------------

I love

Name

I feel

Name

I remember

Name

I believe

Name

I can

Name

I am

Name

I hope

Name

I wonder

Name

I wish

Name

I will

Name

My mom

Name

My dad

Name

When I was little

Name

When I grow up

Name

I always

Name

I never

Name

I dream

Name

I am good at

Name

I know a lot about

Name

Sometimes I

Name

Sometimes I wish

Name

I might

Name

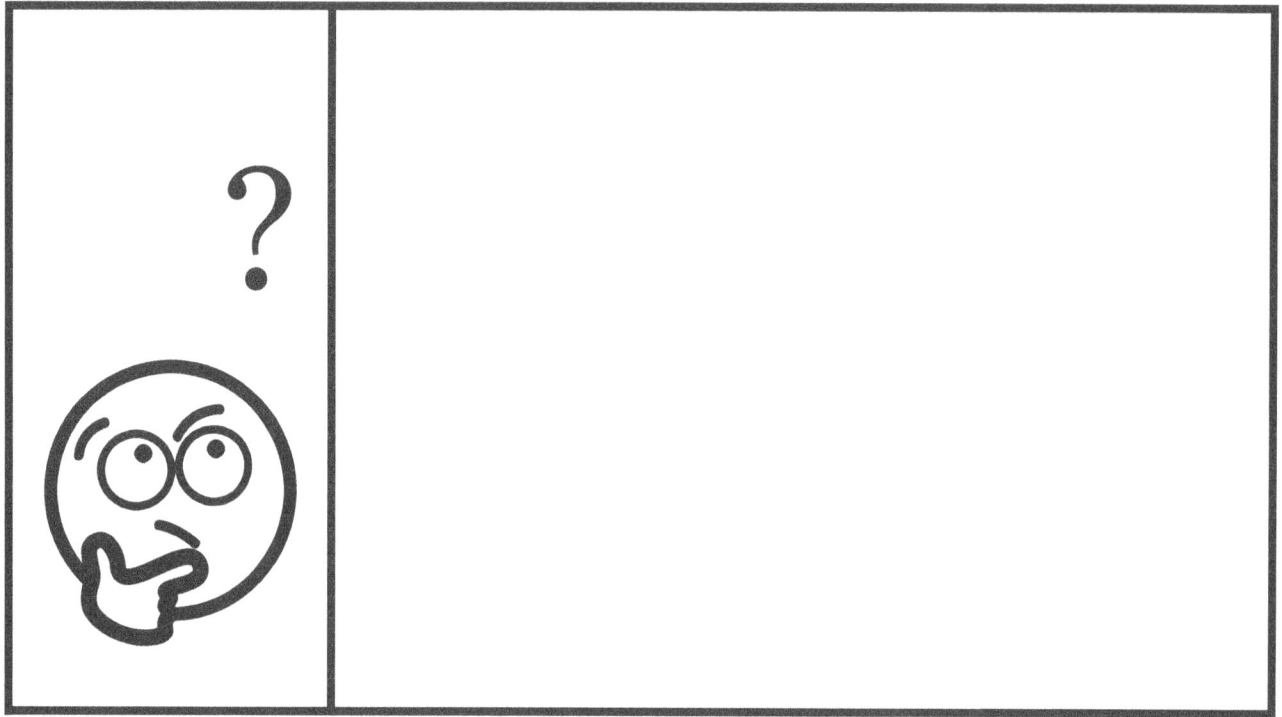

What if

Name

I worry when

Name

I feel bad when

Name

Sometimes

Name

I am happy when

Name

I like to play

Name

I like to go

Name

I love to

Name

I wish I

Name

In the future

Name

At night

Name

In the past

Name _____

I want to

Name

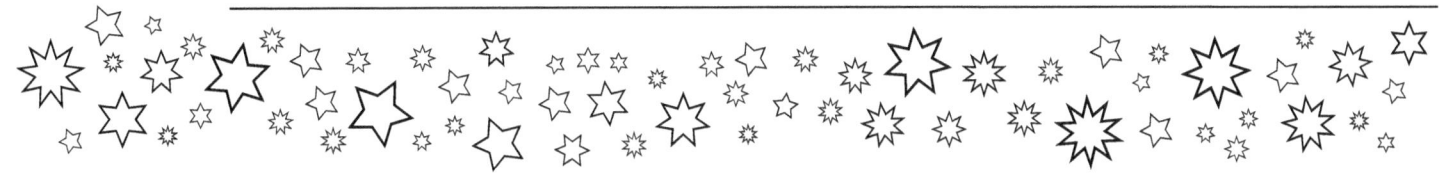

I want to be

Name _____

I must

Name

I like

Name

I should

Name

I felt sorry when

Name

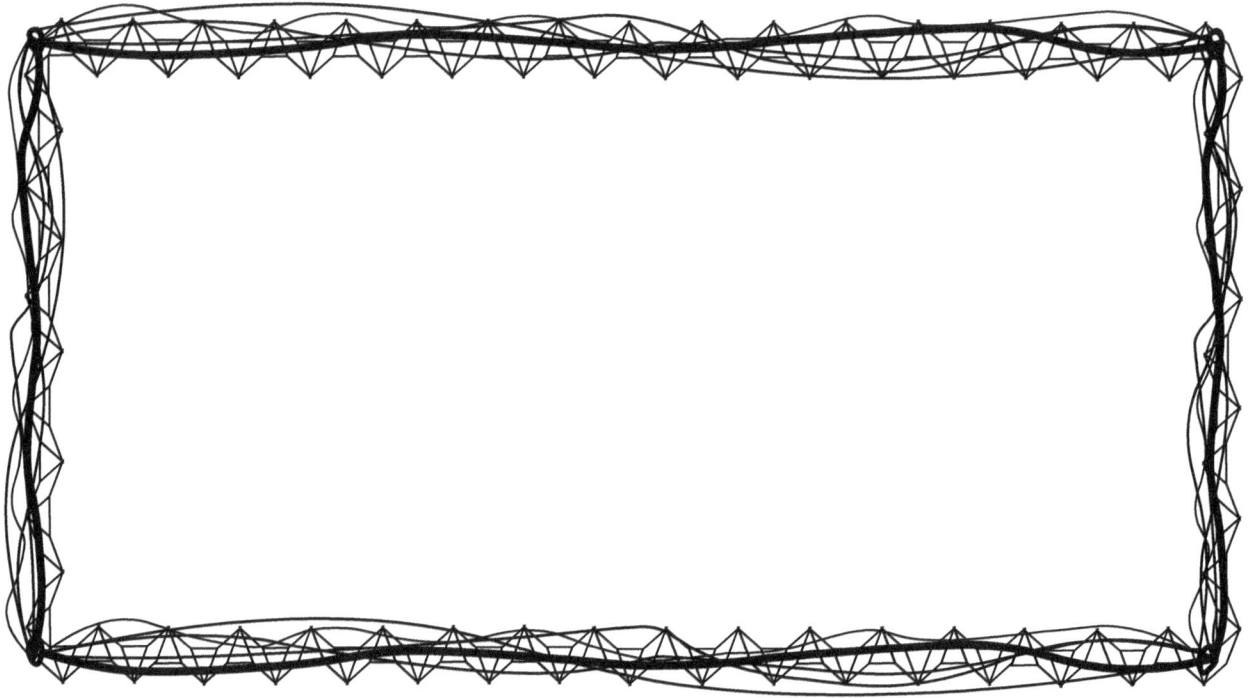

I get mad if

Name

I want

Name

I need

Name

I am feeling

Name

I love my

Name

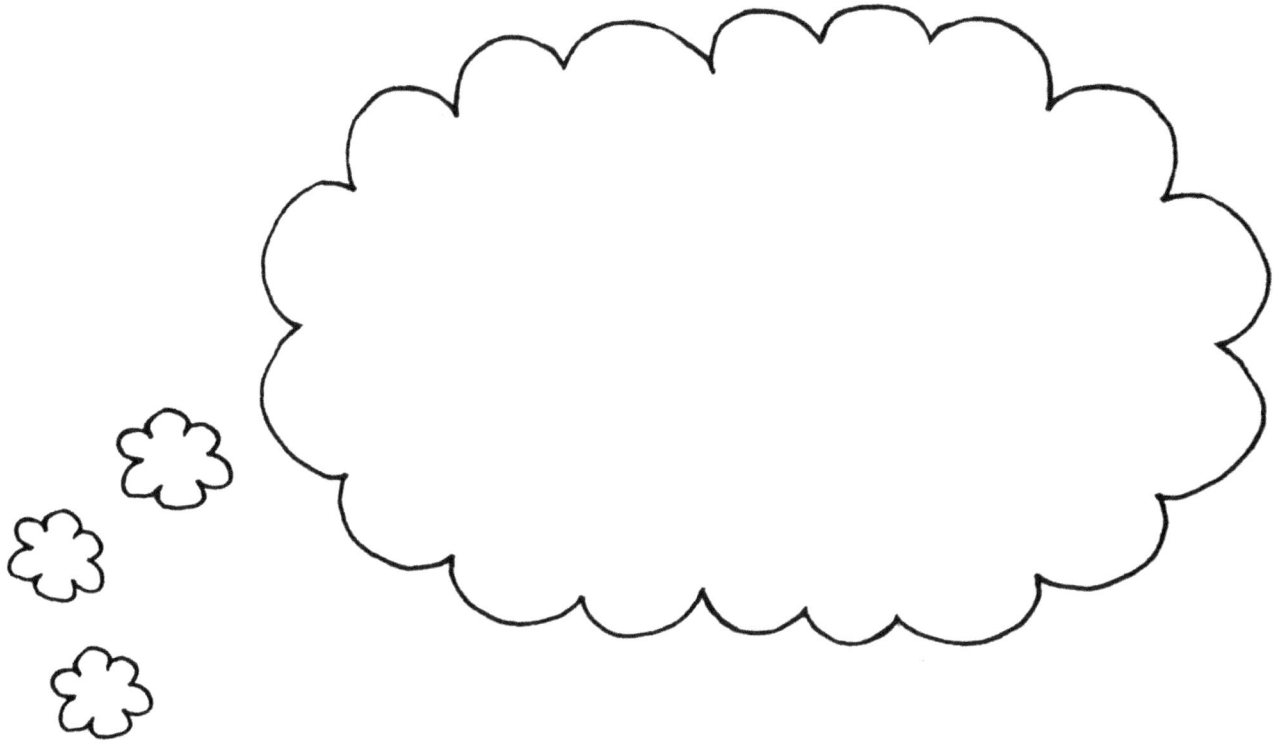

Sometimes I think about

Name

I used to

Name

Every morning

Name

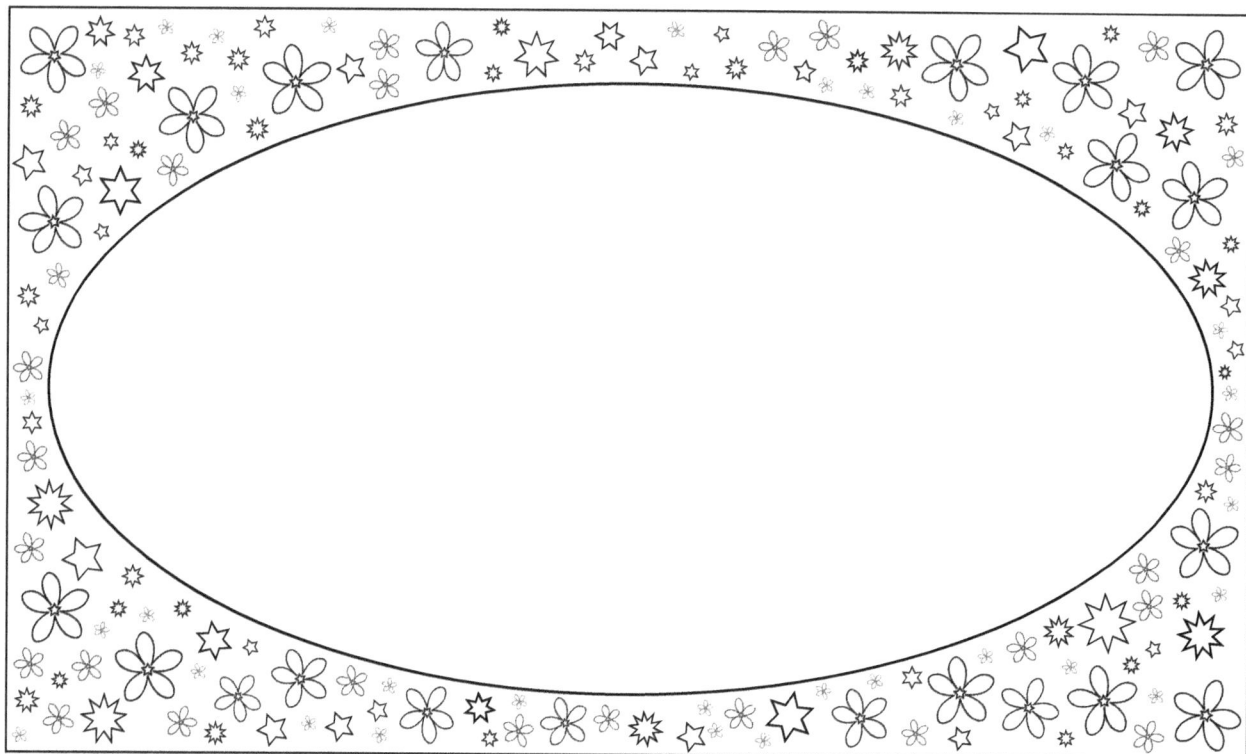

I feel good when

Name

I was so sad when

Name

I do not like it when

Name _____

I get silly when

Name

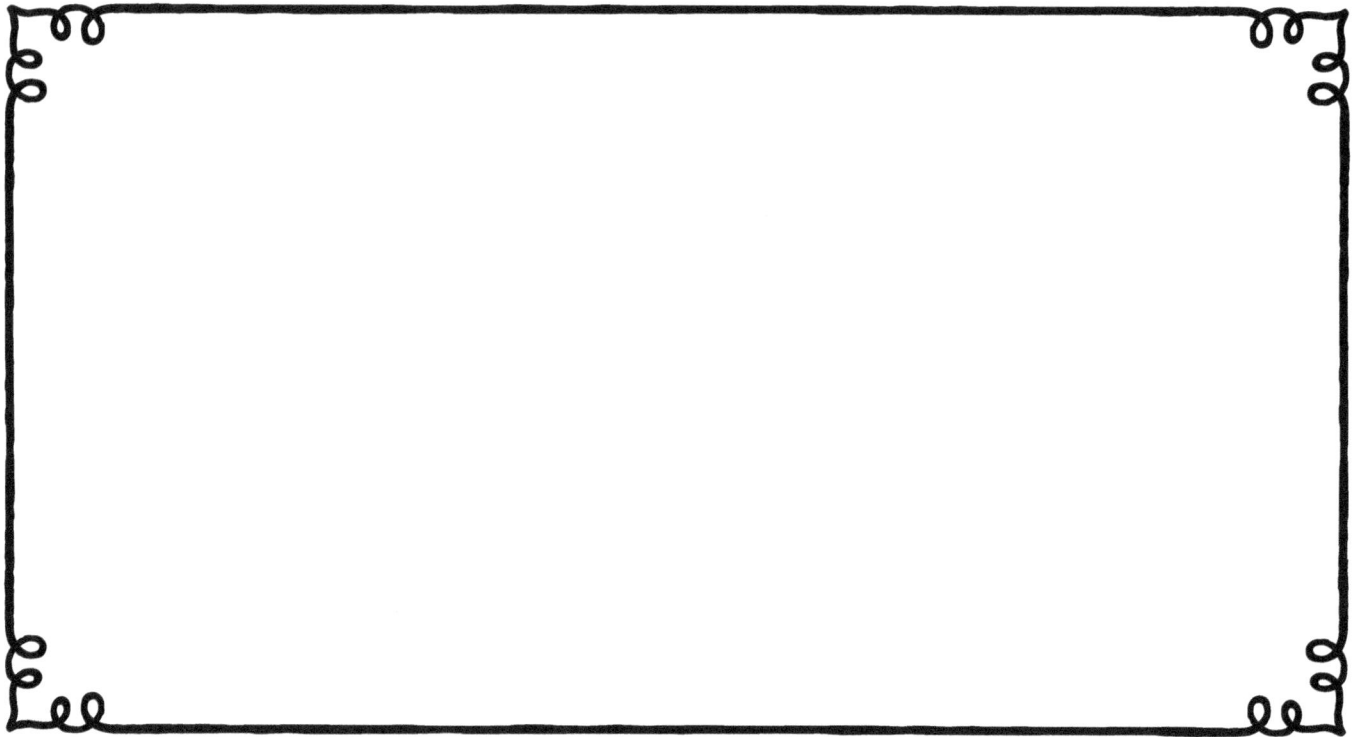

I think it is funny when

Name

At school

Name

At home

Name

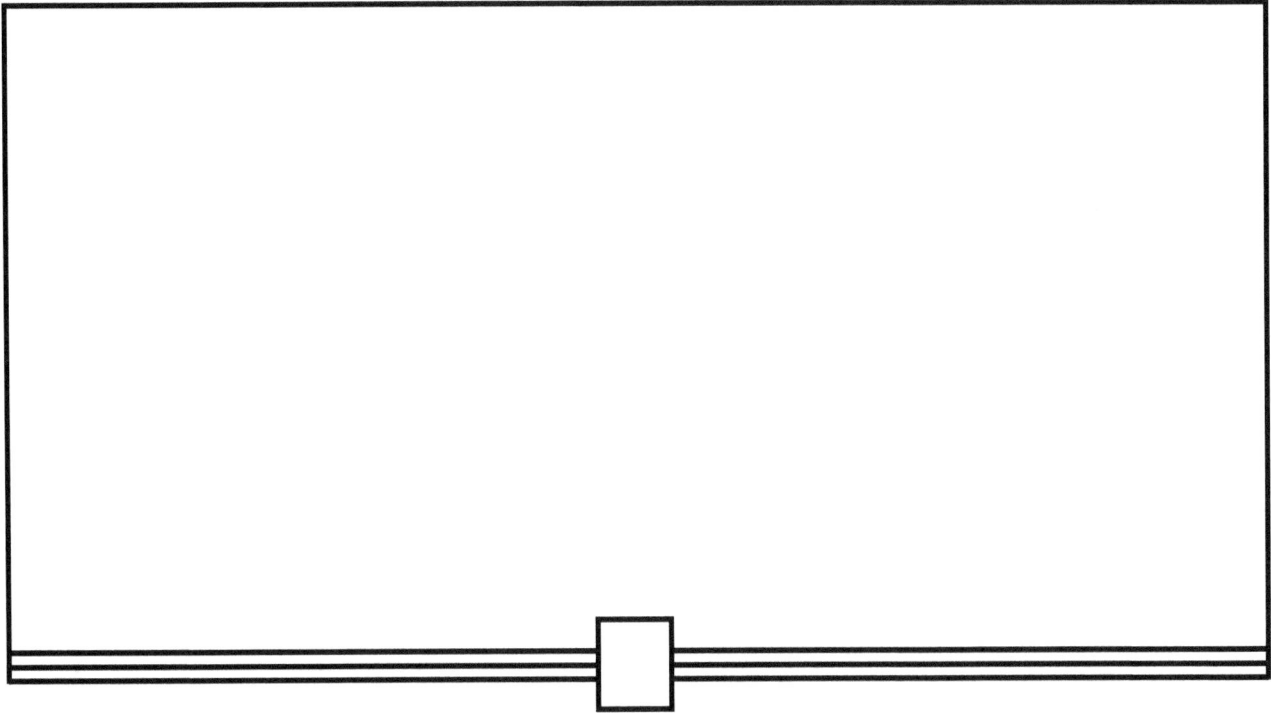

I feel safe when

Name

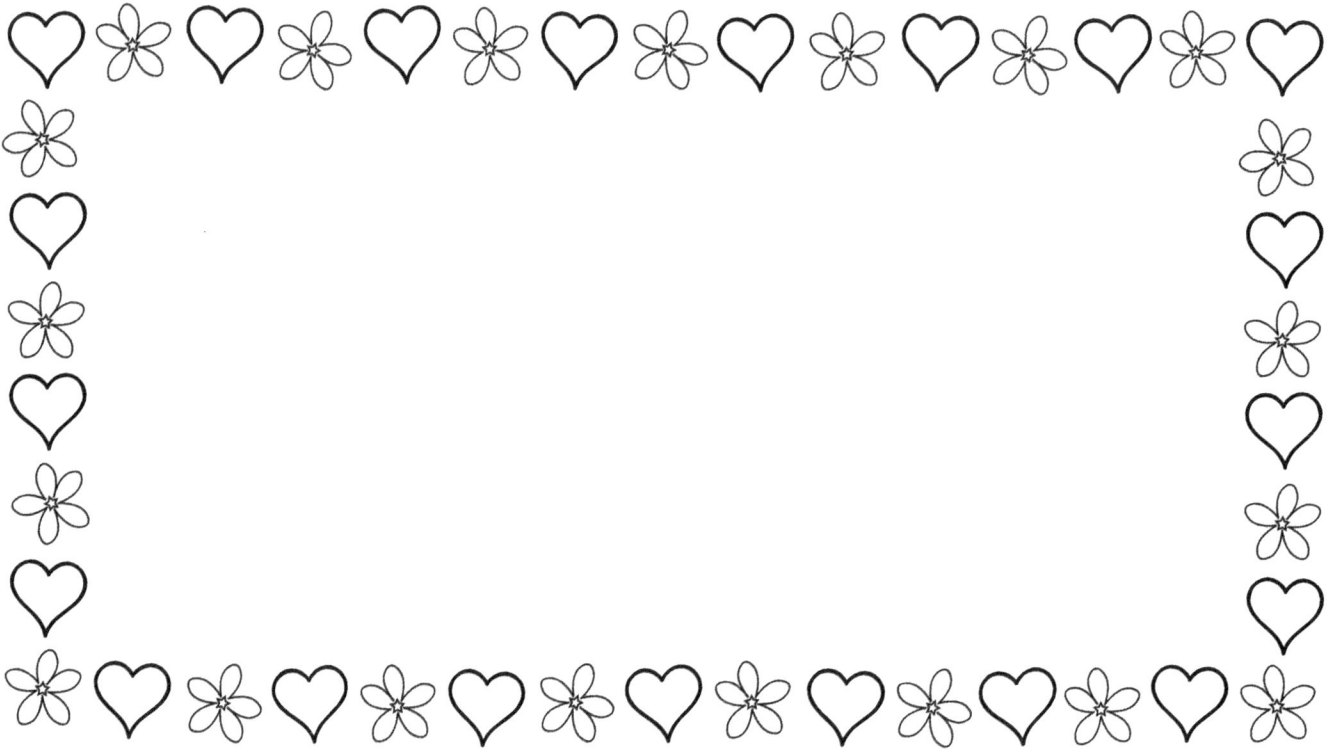

I was happy when

Name

It is fun to

Name

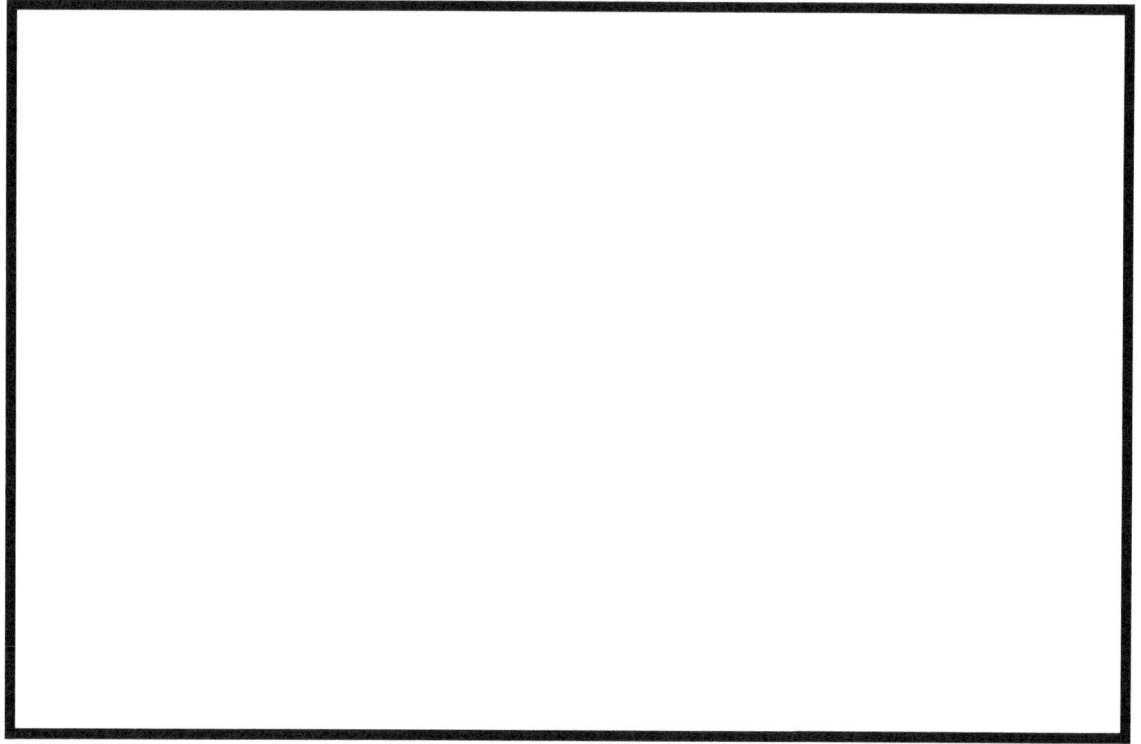

I really like

Name

I try to

Name

I do not like to

Name

I felt unhappy when

Name

I was afraid when

Name

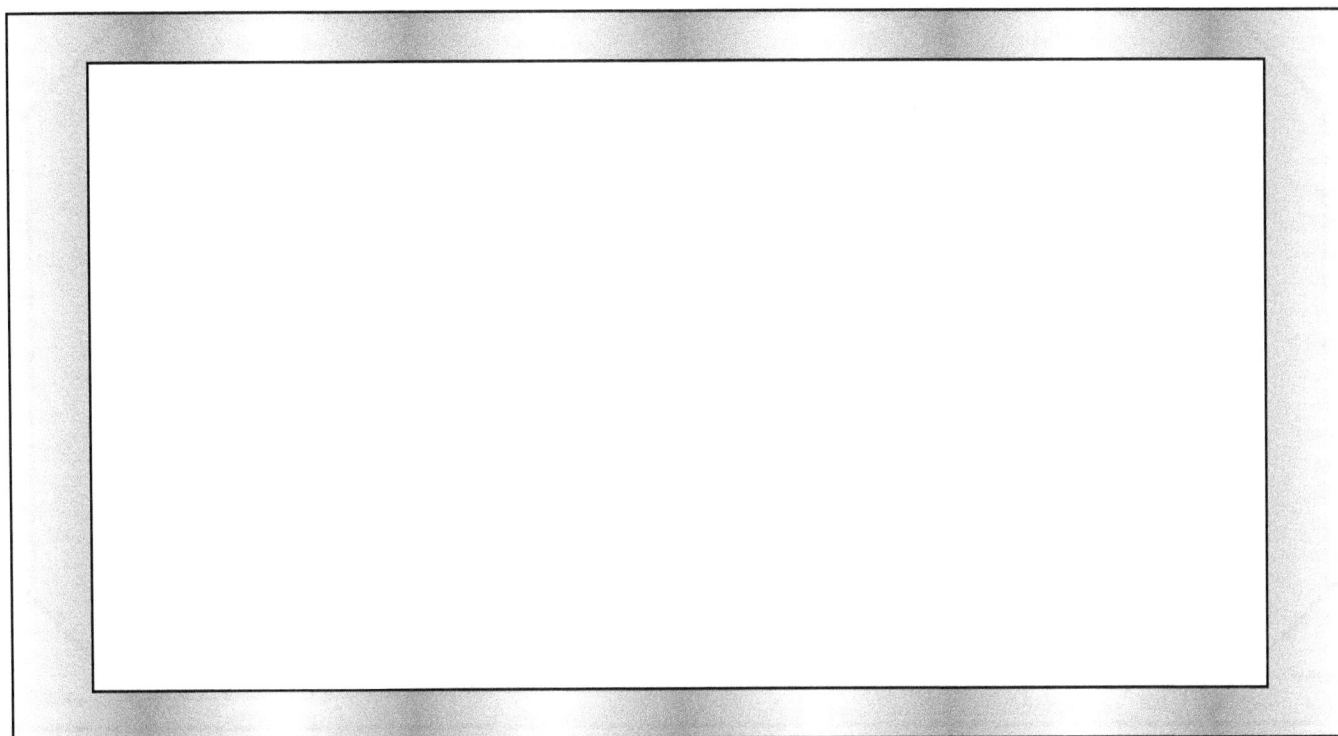

I wish I could

Name

My family

Name

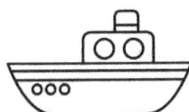

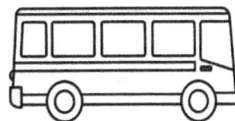

My family likes to go

Name _____

My friends

Name

I went

Name

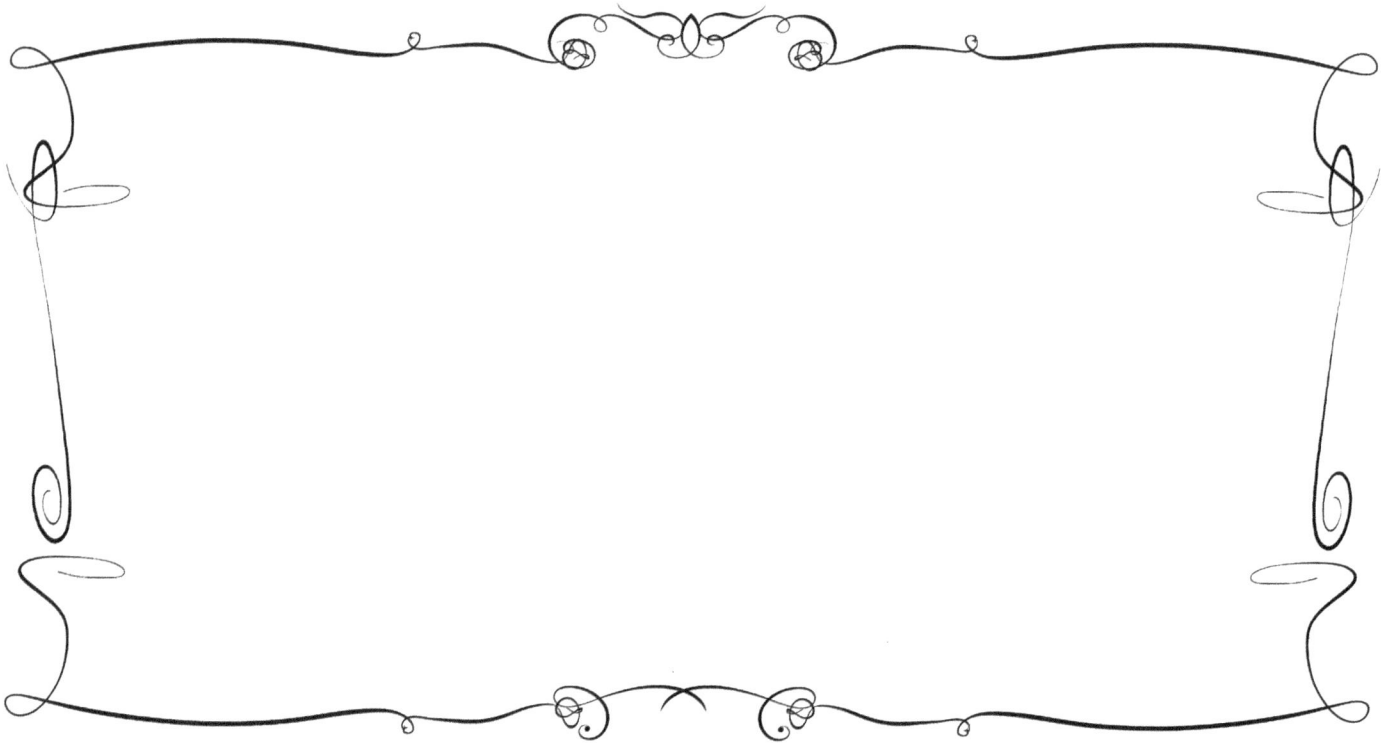

I am thankful for

Name

I am proud of

Name

I want to get better at

Name _____

I want to learn more about

Name

I can be

Name

I am so

Name

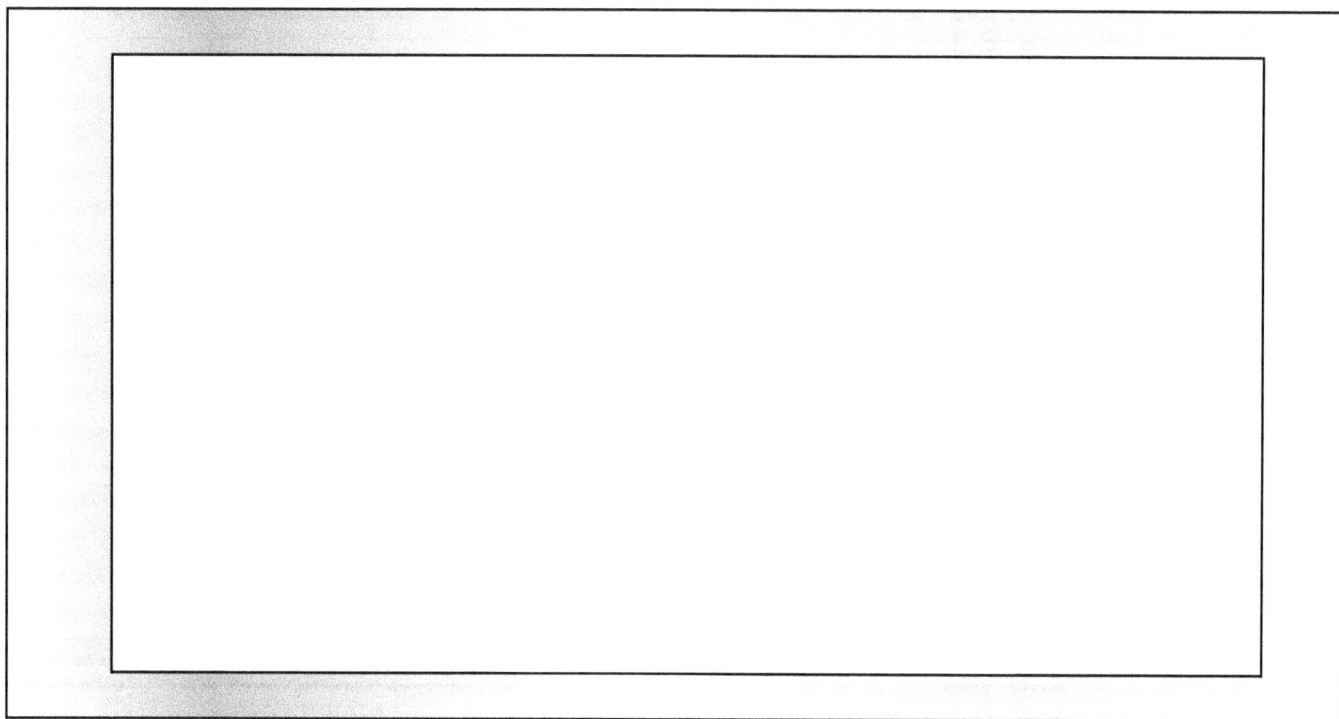

My life

Name

Name

Name

Name

Name

INDEX of FIRST LINES

About the Author

Mark Linley is a public school teacher and curriculum developer with over 20 years of experience teaching full time in the primary grades. He is the author of these and many other high quality learning materials, available on Amazon, Barnes and Noble, Teachers Pay teachers, bartlebysbox.com, and other fine online retail establishments.